978-0-9975343-0-6
Copyright © 2016 Sharalyn Morrison-Andrews

All rights reserved. No part of this book may be reproduced or transmitted in any form or by any means, electronic or mechanical, including photocopying, recording, or by any information storage and retrieval system, without permission in writing from the copyright owner.

This book was printed in the United States of America.

Published by Sharalyn Morrison-Andrews
October 2016

This book is dedicated to my Mom and Dad - thank you for always supporting my dreams!

&

In loving memory of my dear friend Suzanne Cohen and sweet Lizzie.

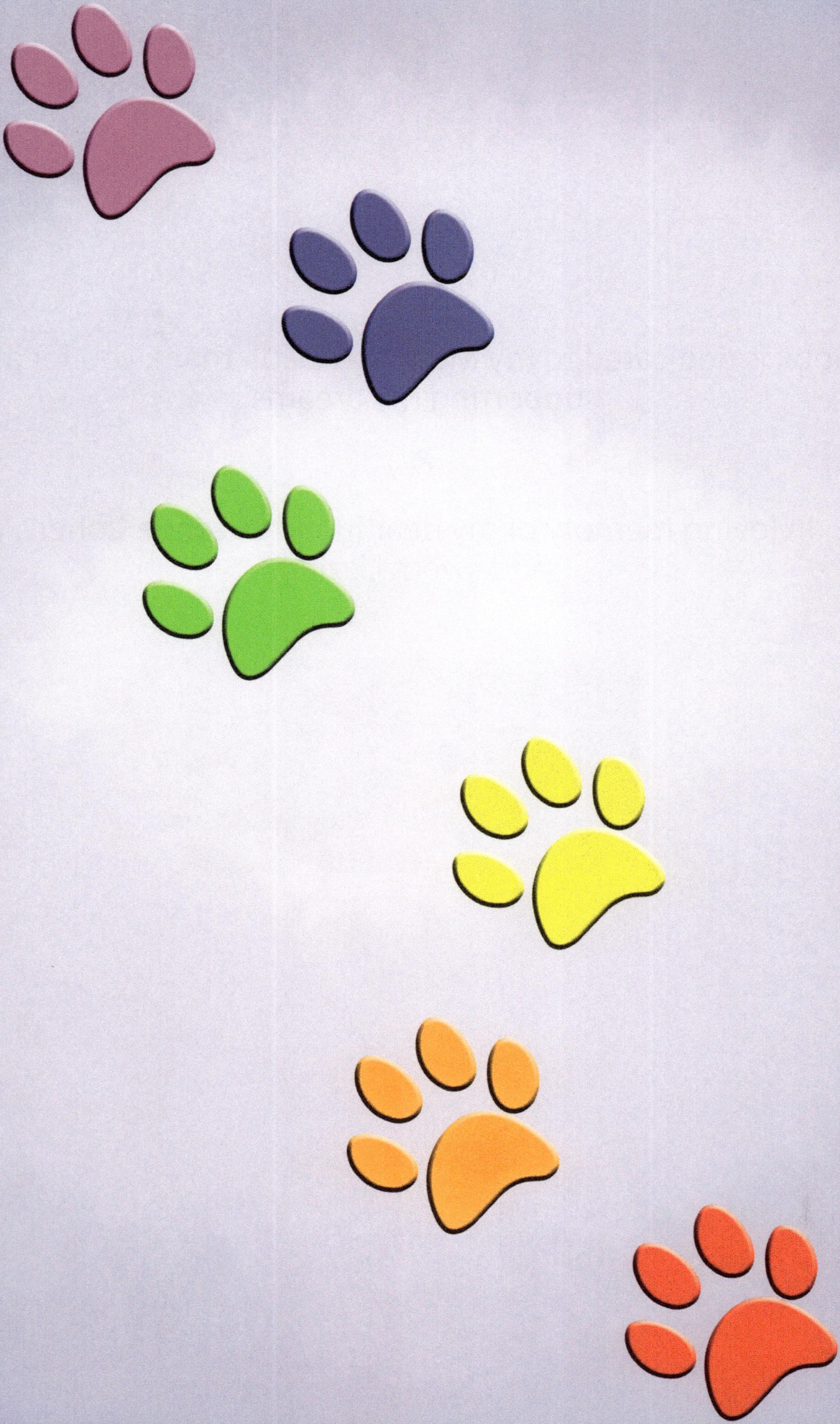

Lizzie's Lesson

by Sharalyn Morrison-Andrews
Illustrated by Lucas Richards

Hello, my name is Lizzie. I live in a small town in Maine. Do you know where Maine is? I like cuddles, carrots and playing with my doggie friends. What do you like?

I have a favorite saying:
"When things change and I feel sad,
I will always remember good comes from bad."

Whenever something happens that makes me sad,
I say this saying and it helps me feel better.

Do you have a best friend? I have two! My best buddies are Max and Maggie.

When they lived next door to me, we used to play together every day. We played games like hide and seek, tag and hopscotch.

Sometimes we would make up and recite silly rhymes: "Off to play, off to play, we are going to have a fun and exciting day!"

What games do you play with your friends?

Max and Maggie are my best friends forever. One day, their dad told us he had a new job and the family was going to move far away to a place called Portland, a city in southern Maine.

Max, Maggie and I were very sad at the thought of being apart!

Then we said:
"When things change and we feel sad,
we will always remember good comes from bad."

Good things did come from Max and Maggie moving away. The Dawson family moved into the house where Max and Maggie used to live.

They have a dog Baxter and a cat Sylvester who are my new friends, and now we play together all the time.

Another great thing that happened? I got to visit Max and Maggie.

I had never been to Portland before.
When I went to visit them, I got to ride on a train for the first time.

It was wonderful to see my best friends again.
We had a stupendous visit and we explored all over the city.

We went shopping and had lunch in the Old Port area. The shops and restaurants are in old warehouses that used to store cargo from the ships that sailed into Portland a long time ago.

We rode a ferry to Peaks Island and had ice cream.

At Fort Williams Park, we flew kites and I saw my first lighthouse, the Portland Head Light. Did you know that it is the oldest lighthouse in Maine?

In the evening, we had a picnic in Fort Allen Park while listening to a concert and dancing to the music.

I was sad when Max and Maggie moved away, but many good things have happened because of it.

Who is your favorite teacher? I can't decide who mine is.

Last year, Ms. Byron was my teacher. I loved to go to school because Ms. Byron made it so much fun to learn new things.

I enjoyed spending the day with all of my classmates. We worked enthusiastically to learn our lessons so Ms. Byron would be proud of us.

When it was time for recess, I had many friends to play with.

On the last day of school, I was sad because I would not see all of my classmates every day, and next year I would not have Ms. Byron for my teacher. I said my favorite saying to myself:

"When things change and I feel sad,
I will always remember good comes from bad."

This year, Mr. Choate is my teacher. I have never had a man for a teacher, but he is very nice. Once again, I am with my classmates and we are having fun learning the new lessons that Mr. Choate is teaching us.

Mr. Choate really likes sports. When it is time for recess, he plays games with us. I have never had a teacher do that.

2 3 4 5 6 7 8 9 10 11 12 13 14 15 16 17 18 19 20 21 22 23 24

Can you have two favorite teachers?
I cannot decide between Ms. Byron or Mr. Choate.
Who would you choose?

One day, while walking in the park with my mommy, I sprained my paw. I was upset because my paw was very sore and I couldn't walk on it.

My mom took me to my veterinarian, Dr. Davis. He examined my paw and gave me a pretty pink bandage with a heart on it, which made me smile.

Dr. Davis told my mom that I needed to stay off my paw so it would heal.
I felt scared and sad when I hurt my paw. Then I remembered:

"When things change and I feel sad,
I will always remember good comes from bad!"

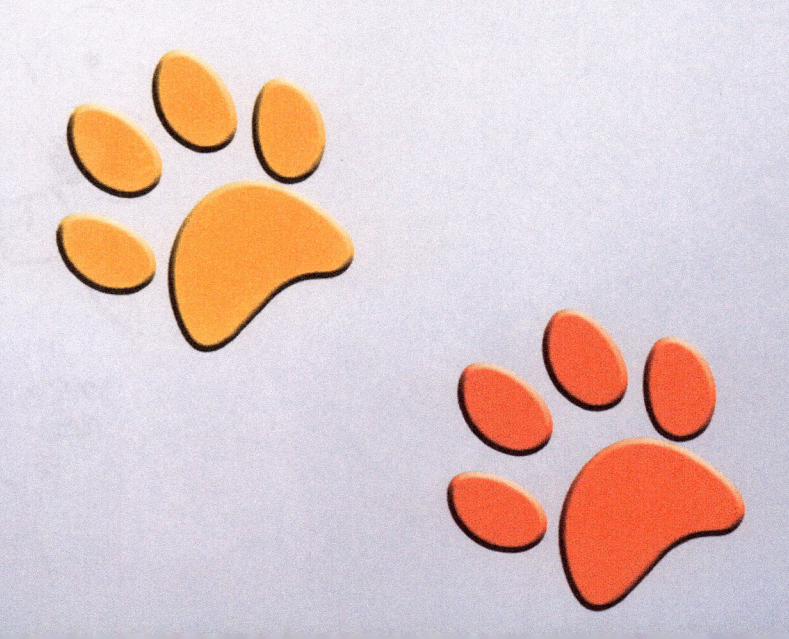

What good could possibly come from an owie you ask?
Well, I was able watch more movies because I couldn't go outside and play.

My mom gave me lots of cuddles and carrots and to help me take my pill,
she put it in peanut butter - YUM!

I am pleased to tell you that my paw is as good as new,
and once again I can run and play.

All of these events were good practice for the time I felt most sad.
It was when my mommy became really, really sick.

At first, I didn't understand that she was sick.
She didn't go to work and she stayed in bed most of the day.

Then, one day, she told me that she didn't feel well and I was sad.

After a few days, my mommy went to the doctor.

When she came home, she told me she would have to go to the hospital once a week to get medicine.

Things were changing and I felt sad.

The days after the trips to get the medicine, my mom would sleep. I was very worried and tried my best to be very good.

I spent most of my days being quiet and sleeping, too.

One day, while cuddling with me, my mommy told me that I was going to stay with her friend, Emily. I didn't want to go. I didn't know Emily very well and I wanted to stay with my mommy.

Things were changing and I was feeling very, very sad.

Emily was very nice. She understood that I was sad and scared. As she cuddled with me, she said:

"Things have changed and you feel sad, but always remember, good comes from bad."

How did Emily know that was my favorite saying? From that moment, I knew that many good things were going to happen. Emily made me feel very safe and special. She planned activities so I would not have time to think about my sick mommy.

We went for long walks on the beach.
There were always other dogs there. I didn't miss my friends too much because there was always someone to run and play with.

Emily's favorite snack was carrots, just like me! She had a refrigerator full of them and would share them with me all day long.

We went for long rides in the car and we visited with Emily's mom and dad.

They became my "new grandparents."

Thelma is Emily's neighbor and she loves little doggies.

Whenever Emily and I went for a walk, I always tried to go to see Thelma because she had special treats for me.

Emily made me feel very comfortable in her home. She made certain that every day we had plenty of "prime time cuddle time."

Most of all, Emily took me to visit with my mommy often.
I was always so happy to see her and spend time with her.

When it was time to leave, I always felt a little sad, but it was
nice to go back to Emily's home, too.

While my mommy was sick and I was home with her, I felt that I needed to
be quiet and not bother her. At Emily's, I was able to run and play more.

Slowly, the medicine began to make my mom feel better and I was able to go back home.

I am very happy to be home and with my mom again.

I miss Emily and know that she misses me, too, because she often invites me for sleepovers.

Now, my days are back to the way they used to be, but I know the next time when things change, I will remember my favorite saying. Can you say it with me?

"When things change and I feel sad,
I will always remember good comes from bad."

Casco Bay

Portland

South Portland

*Great
Diamond*

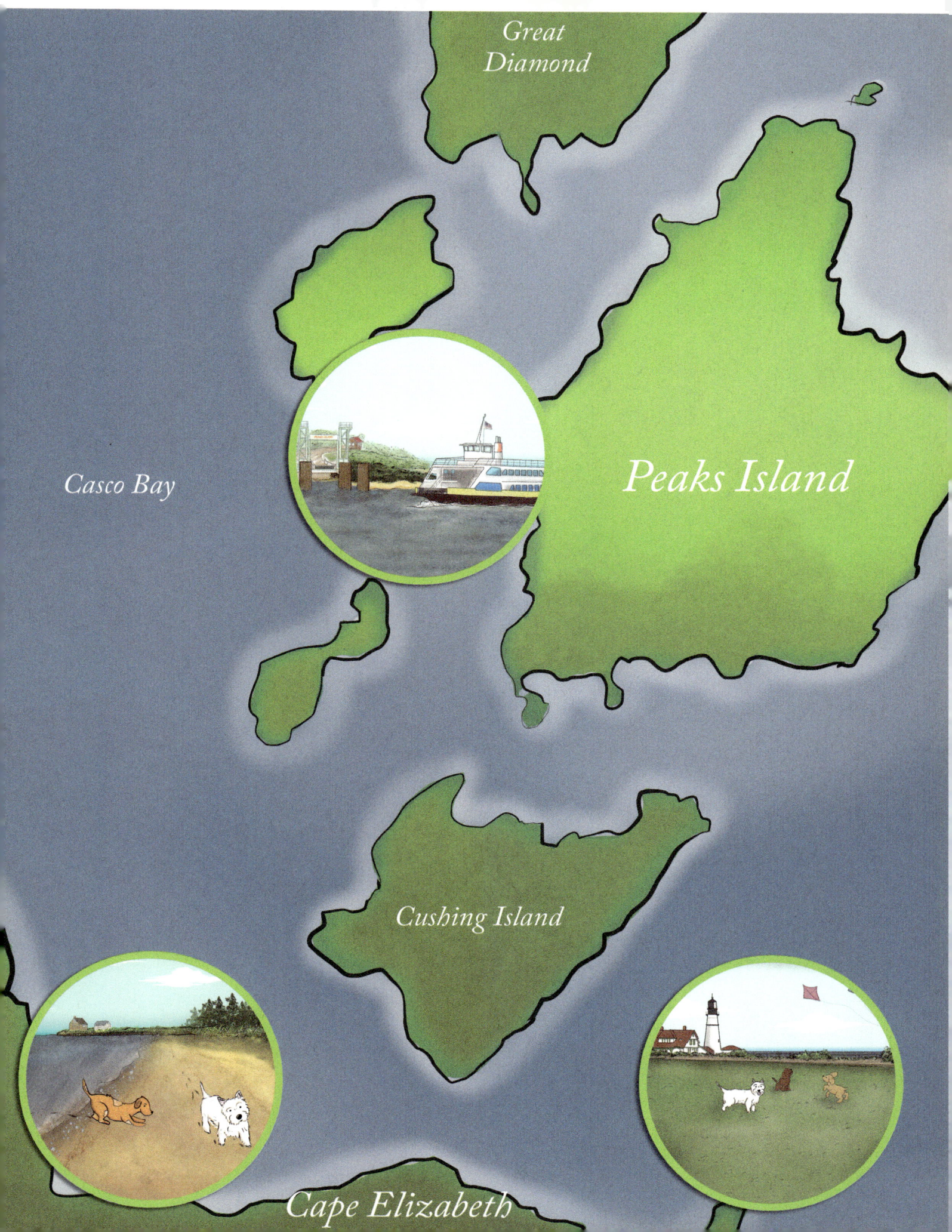

Casco Bay

Peaks Island

Cushing Island

Cape Elizabeth

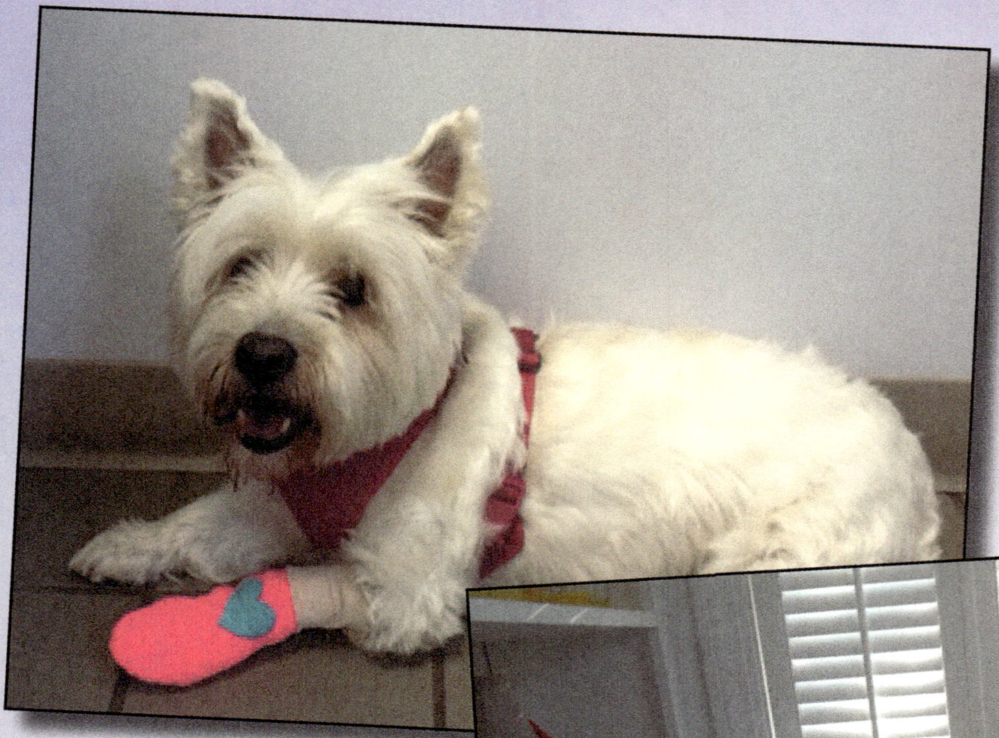

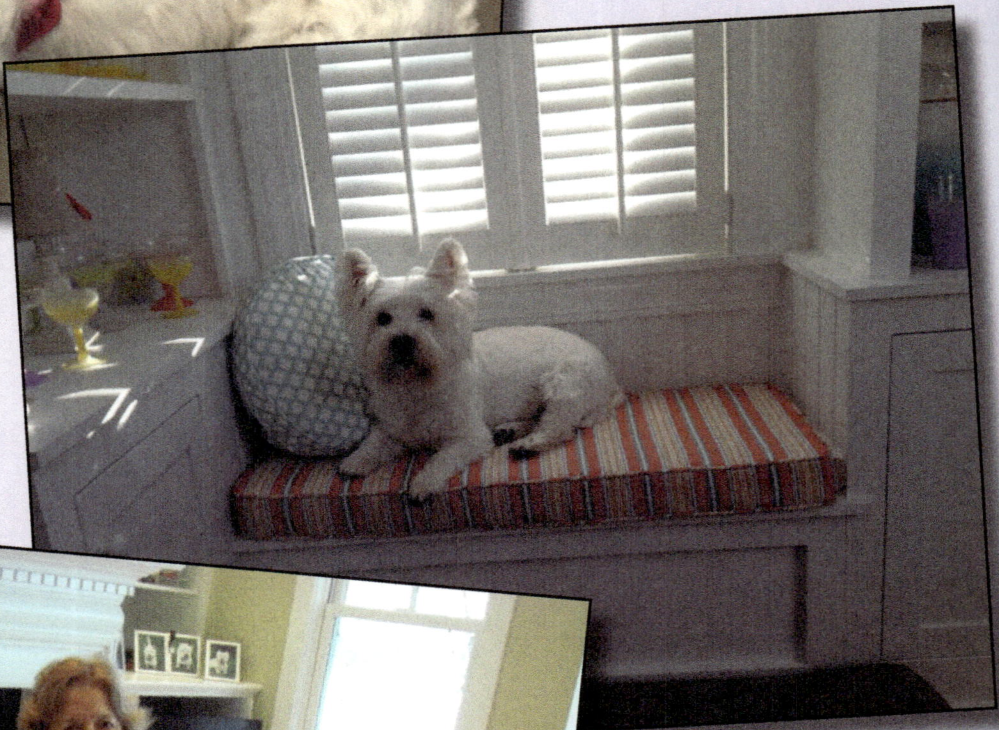

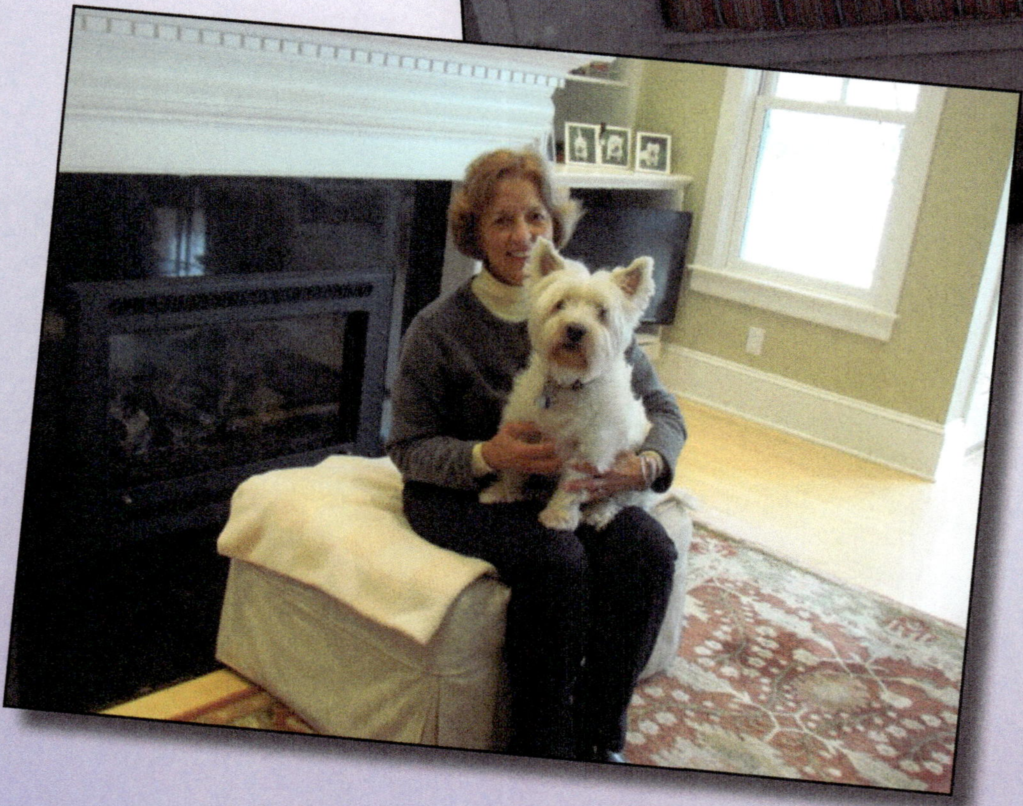

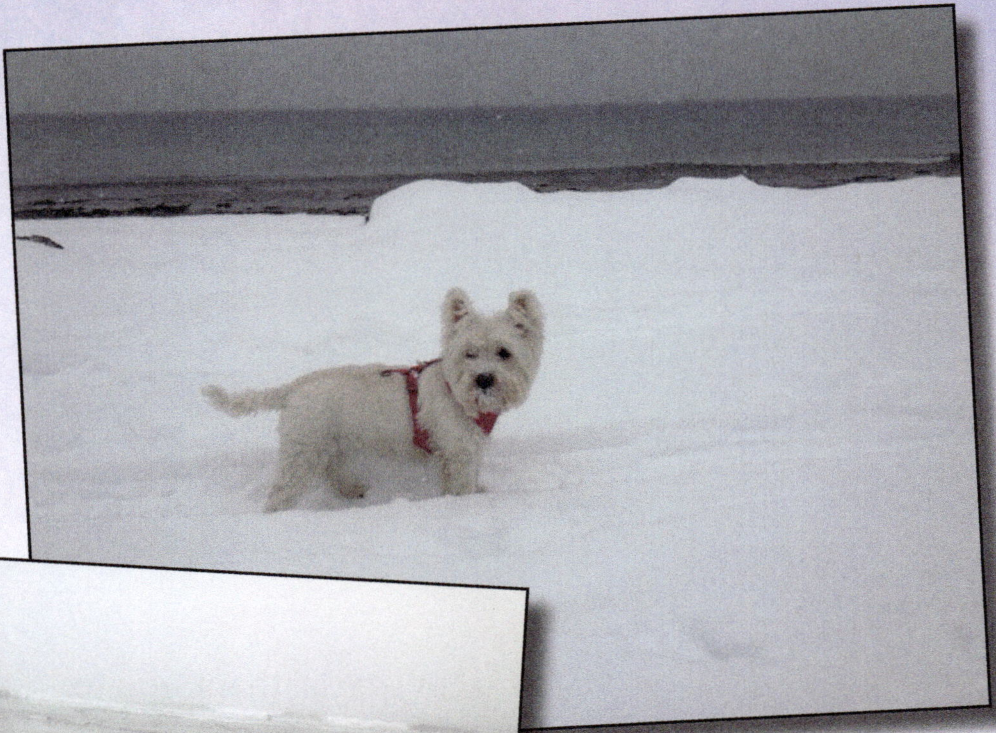

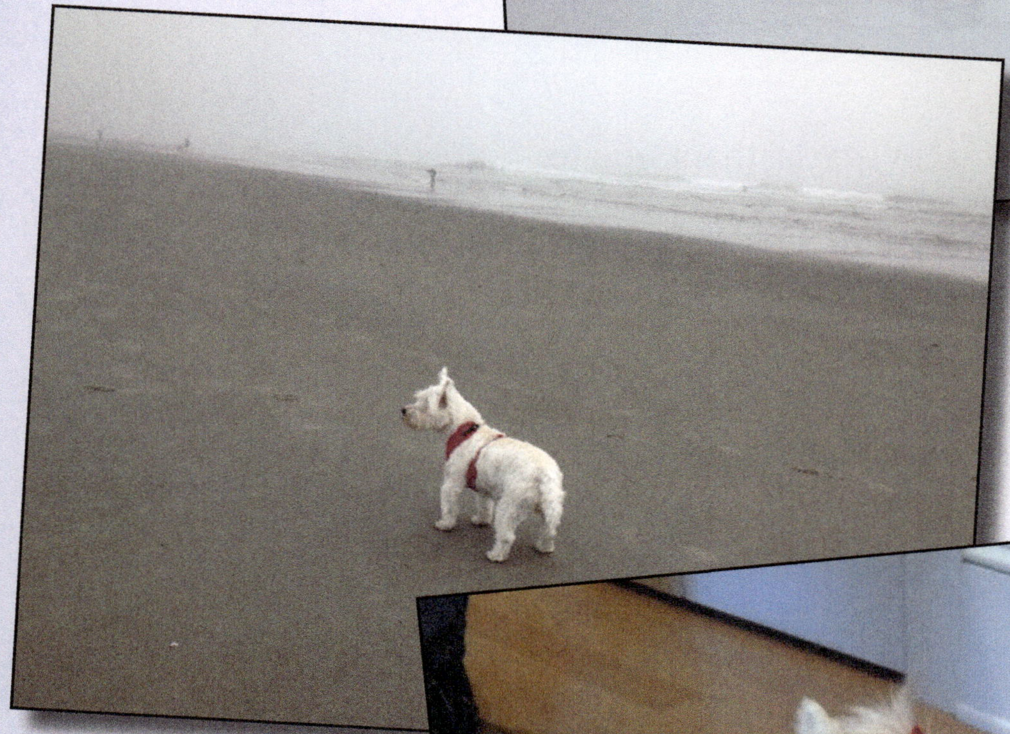

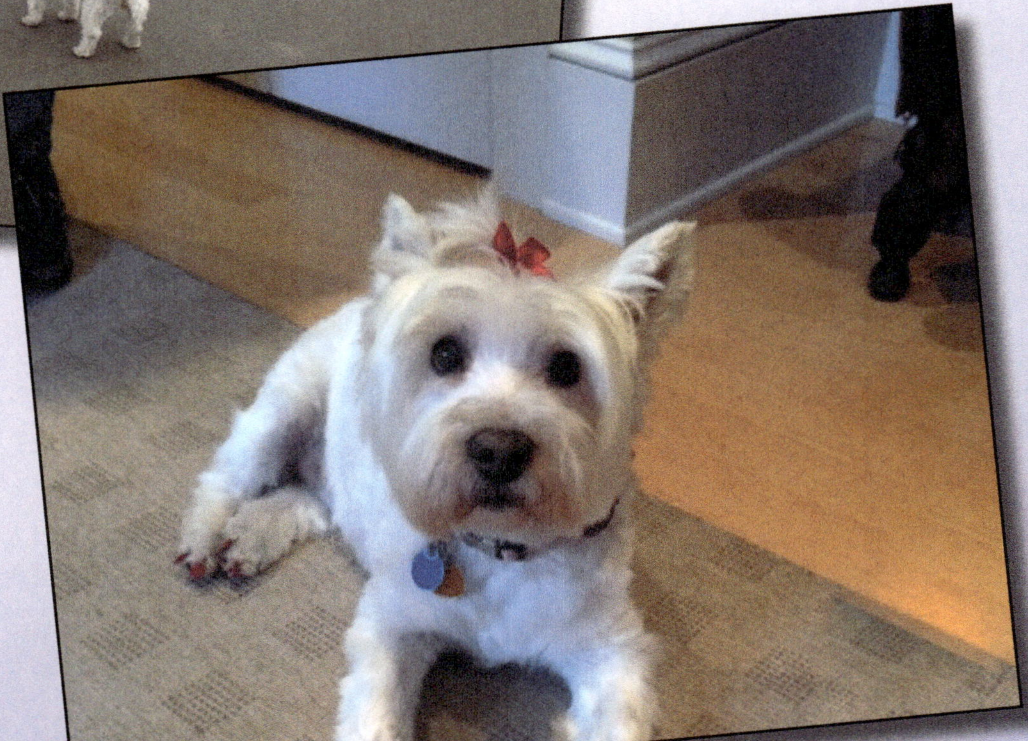

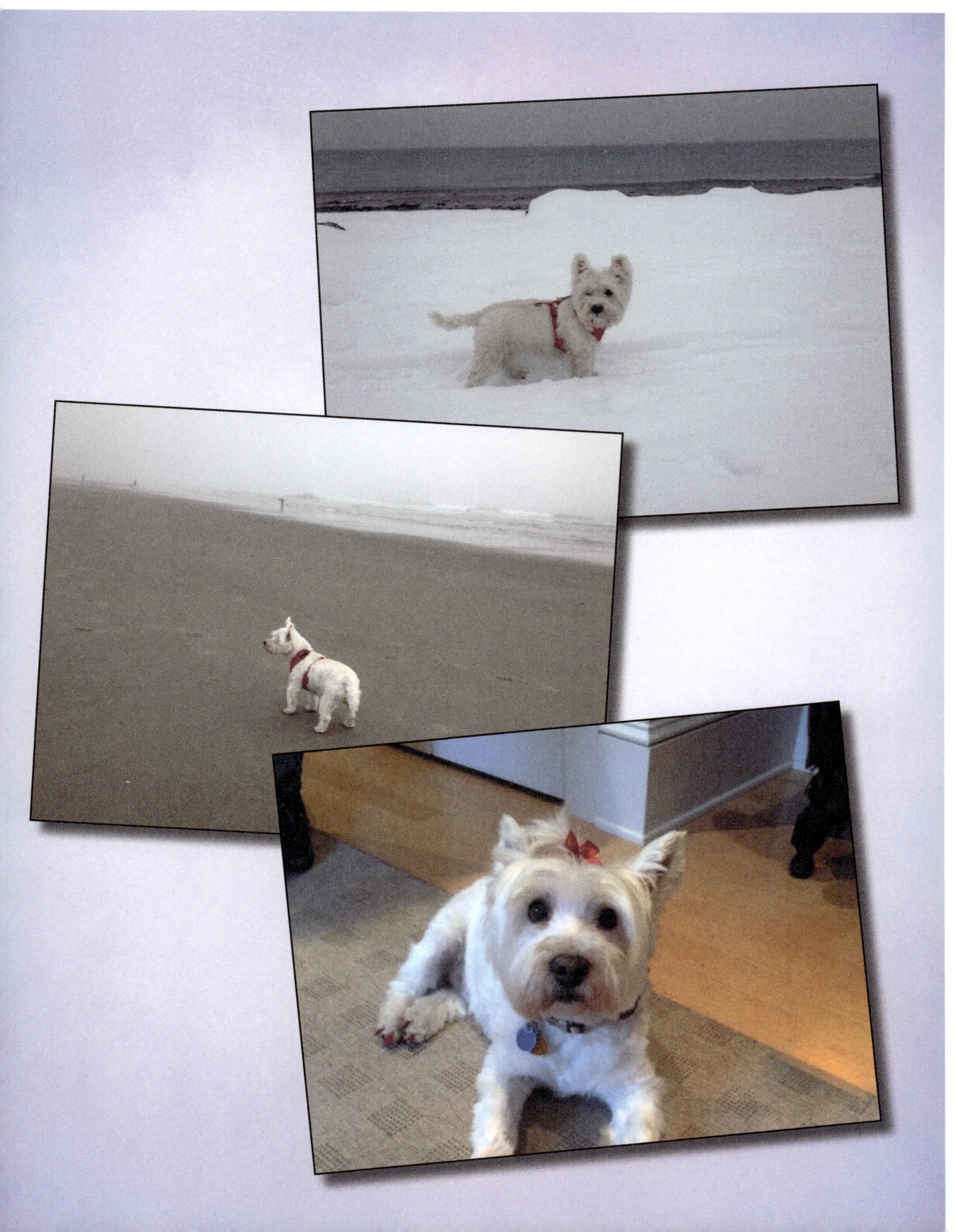

A special thank you to:

Nathan Curtis and Jenica Frazier for their willingness to share their journey of living with a parent who was ill.

&

Lori Ferguson - for the times words escaped me!
www.writerloriferguson.com

Sharalyn grew up in Hallowell, Maine and was bitten by the "travel bug" at a very young age. While she loved to travel as a young woman, it was her marriage to David, whose job frequently takes them out of the country, that made travel a vital part of her life.

Over the years, Sharalyn has enjoyed writing by keeping a journal and, most recently, a blog. Her new interest is writing children's books about dogs she has known and the important life messages they impart to children. When not traveling, Sharalyn and her husband make their home in Maine.

You can follow Sharalyn on her website at www.sharlaynlovesanimals.com.

Lucas grew up in Cape Elizabeth, Maine. His aptitude as an artist emerged early in life. One could find him drawing on anything he could reach in his family's home. His studies and passion for travel have allowed him to visit some of the world's best art museums, experiences that influence his style today.

You can follow Lucas at on his website at www.Lucas-Richards.com